MY 1ST BOOK OF
BABY ANIMALS

Amazon Page : amazon.com/author/rainbowartsstudio
Email : sara.rainbowartsstudio@gmail.com
IG : rainbow_artsstudio

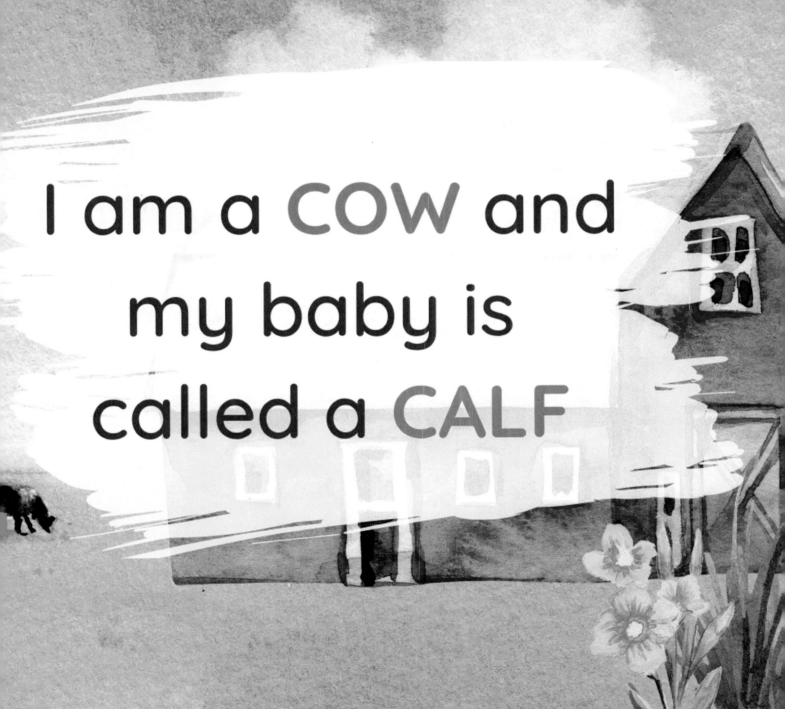

I am a **COW** and my baby is called a **CALF**

I am a **HORSE** and my baby is called a **FOAL**

I am a **SHEEP** and my baby is called a **LAMB**

I am a **DOG** and my baby is called a **PUPPY**

I am a **CAT** and my baby is called a **KITTEN**

I am a **GOAT** and my baby is called a **KID**

I am a HEN and my baby is called a CHICK

I am a **FROG** and my baby is called a **TADPOLE**

I am a **RABBIT** and my baby is called a **BUNNY**

I am a DUCK and my baby is called a DUCKLING

I am a **TURTLE** and my baby is called a **HATCHLING**

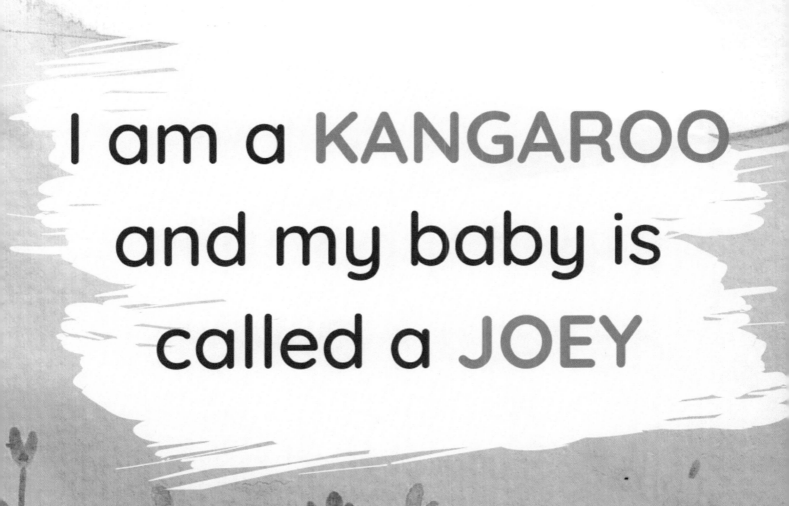

I am a KANGAROO and my baby is called a JOEY

I am a **FLAMINGO** and my baby is called a **CHICK**

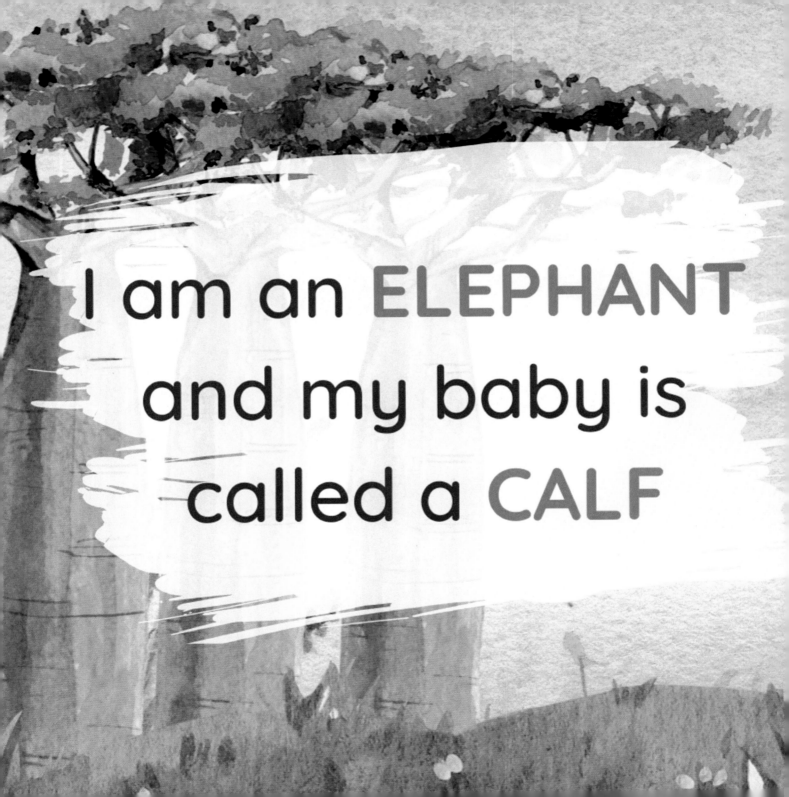

I am an ELEPHANT and my baby is called a CALF

I am an OWL and my baby is called an OWLET

I am a **DEER** and my baby is called a **FAWN**

I am a PENGUIN and my baby is called a CHICK

I am a PANDA and my baby is called a CUB

I am a FOX and my baby is called a KIT

I am a **HIPPO** and my baby is called a **CALF**

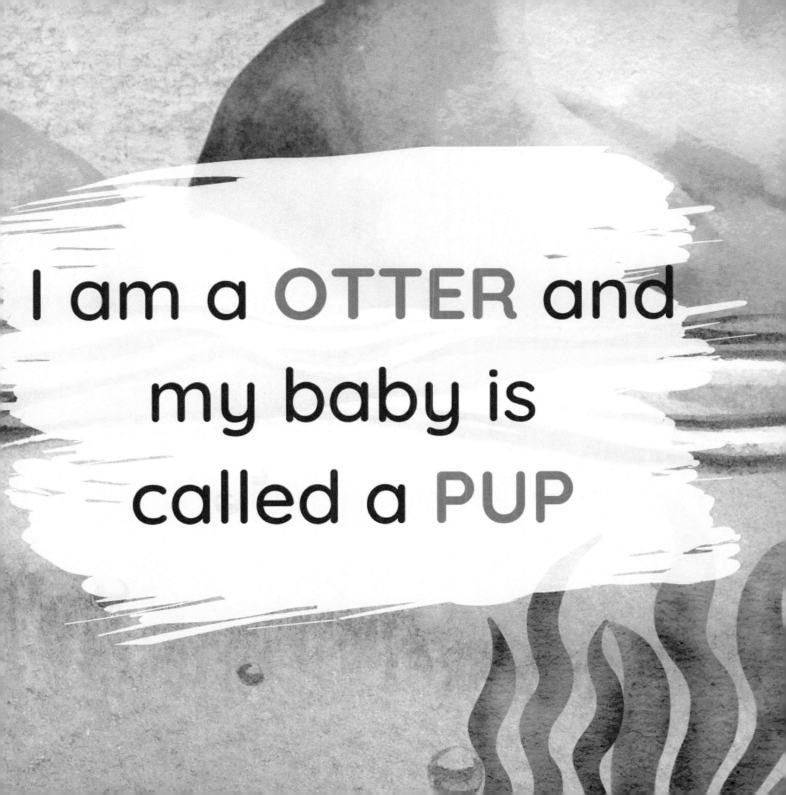

I am a OTTER and my baby is called a PUP

I am a **LION** and my baby is called a **CUB**

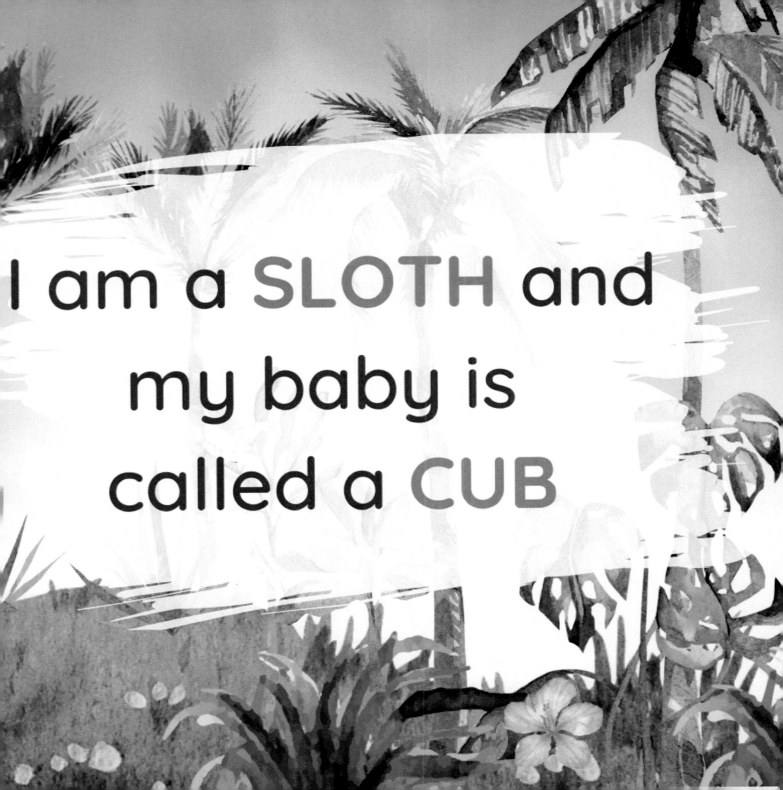

I am a SLOTH and my baby is called a CUB

We are a small publishing house
and if you enjoyed this book please
leave us a review. Your feedback
matters to us!

Made in United States
Orlando, FL
28 April 2022

17296581R00029